NOT JUST ANOTHER Scale Book

10 Innovative Piano Solos
Using Major and Minor Scales

Mike Springer

Practicing scales is usually not at the top of students' "to do" lists. Yet, the importance of such practice cannot be overstated. A student with a good working knowledge and mastery of scales has a distinct advantage.

Not Just Another Scale Book was written to inspire students to practice scales. Disguised within each piece in this book are scales—sometimes ascending, sometimes descending—in one or both hands. Careful attention has been given to the fingering of the scales, and excerpts for sight-reading precede the pieces. The scale patterns found within each piece will help students recognize, more quickly and easily, similar patterns found in standard literature.

What makes this book truly different, however, is the accompanying compact disc that features innovative and fun orchestrated background tracks for all of the scales and solos in the book. For each solo, there are three different versions of the background. The first version (Performance Model) is a complete performance of the piece featuring the piano solo with orchestrated background. The second version (Practice Tempo) is the orchestrated background, minus the solo part, at a slower tempo designed to be used for practice purposes. The third version (Performance Tempo) is the orchestrated background, minus the solo part, at the performance tempo. This third version is designed to be used for performance.

Not Just Another Scale Book is simply that—not just another book of scales and pieces. Instead, it presents a fun way to reinforce the learning of scales with pieces that offer performance options and are sure to be among students' favorites.

Contents

ISBN-10: 0-7390-4240-8
ISBN-13: 978-0-7390-4240-3

C Major (no sharps or flats)

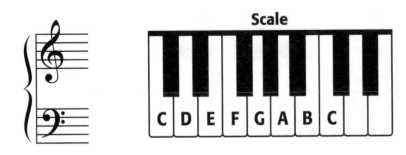

One-Octave Scale

RH: 1 2 3 1 2 3 4 5
LH: 5 4 3 2 1 3 2 1

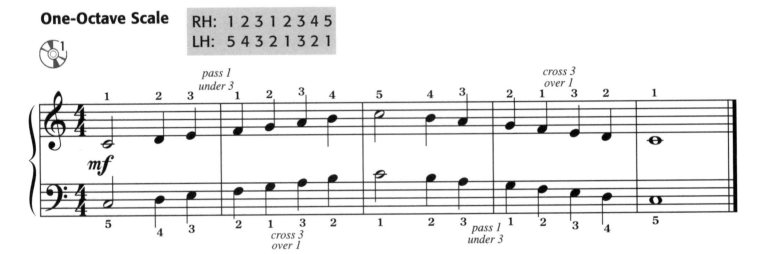

Scale Preparation for Boogie Woogie Rock (pp. 4–5)

Play the examples 3 times each day.

A Minor (no sharps or flats)

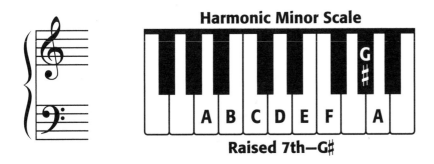

One-Octave Scale

RH: 1 2 3 1 2 3 4 5
LH: 5 4 3 2 1 3 2 1

A dot (•) above a fingering indicates a black key.

Scale Preparation for Secret Mission (pp. 6–7)

Play the examples 3 times each day.

1. (mm. 1–2)

2. (mm. 12–15)

3. (mm. 5–6)

4. (mm. 19–21)

Boogie Woogie Rock

3 Performance Model
4 Practice Tempo (♩ = 126)
5 Performance Tempo (♩ = 144)

Mike Springer

Secret Mission

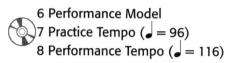

6 Performance Model
7 Practice Tempo ($\bullet$ = 96)
8 Performance Tempo ($\bullet$ = 116)

Mike Springer

Moderately fast and sneaky

F Major (1 flat—B♭)

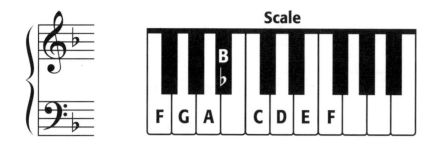

Scale

One-Octave Scale

RH: 1 2 3 4̇ 1 2 3 4   A dot (•) above a fingering
LH: 5 4 3 2 1 3 2 1   indicates a black key.

Scale Preparation for Falling Leaves (pp. 10–11)

Play the examples 3 times each day.

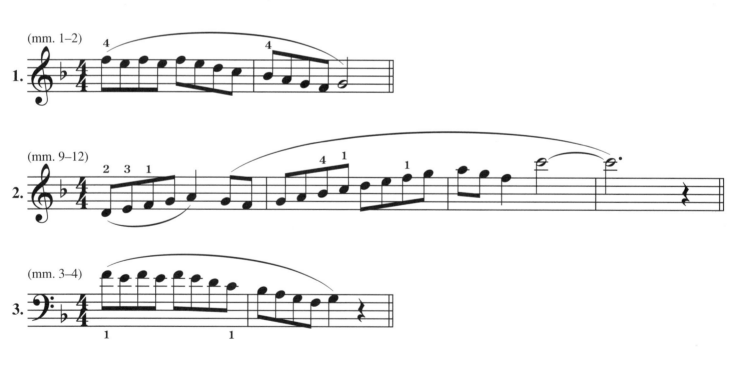

D Minor (1 flat—B♭)

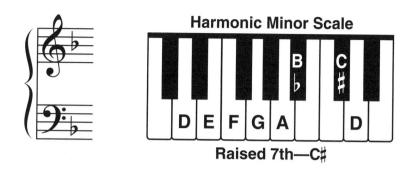

Harmonic Minor Scale

Raised 7th—C♯

One-Octave Scale

RH: 1 2 3 1 2 3̈ 4 5 A dot (•) above a fingering
LH: 5 4 3 2 1 3 2 1 indicates a black key.

Scale Preparation for Midnight Crawl (pp. 12–13)

Play the examples 3 times each day.

(mm. 7–8)

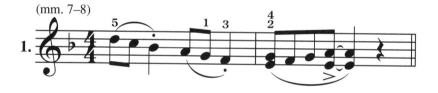

mm. (15–16)

(mm. 1–4)

(mm. 31–32)

* Midnight Crawl uses the melodic form of the D minor scale.

Falling Leaves

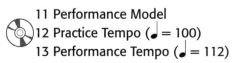

11 Performance Model
12 Practice Tempo ($\quad$ = 100)
13 Performance Tempo ($\quad$ = 112)

Mike Springer

Swiftly and gently

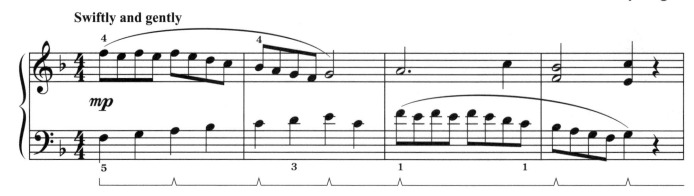

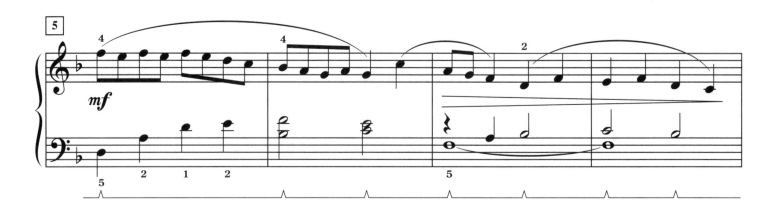

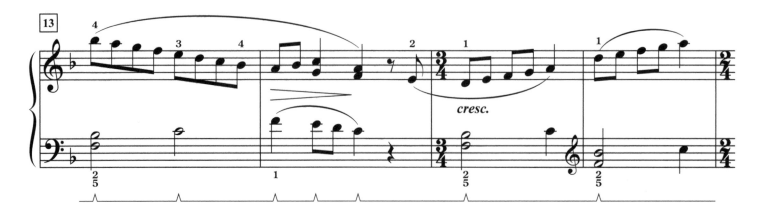

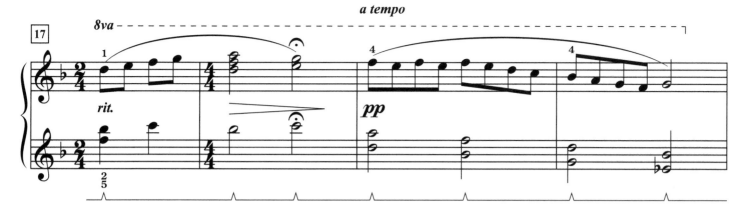

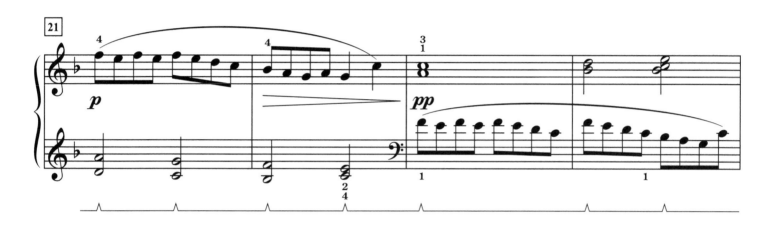

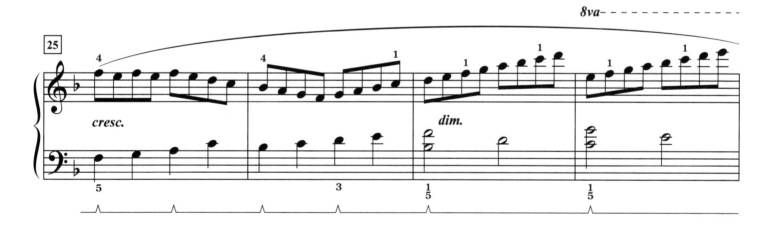

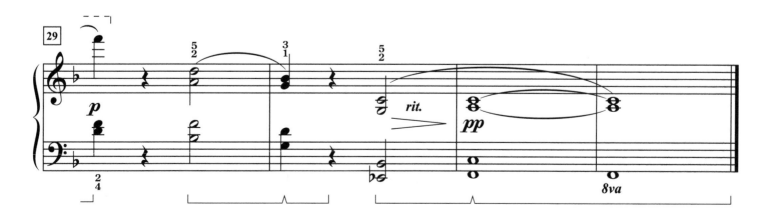

Midnight Crawl

14 Performance Model
15 Practice Tempo (♩ = 112)
16 Performance Tempo (♩ = 126)

Mike Springer

G Major (1 sharp—F♯)

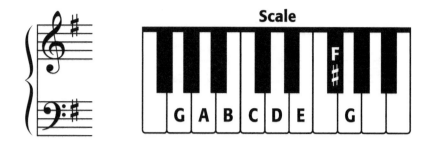

One-Octave Scale

RH: 1 2 3 1 2 3 4 5
LH: 5 4 3 2 1 3 2 1

A dot (•) above a fingering indicates a black key.

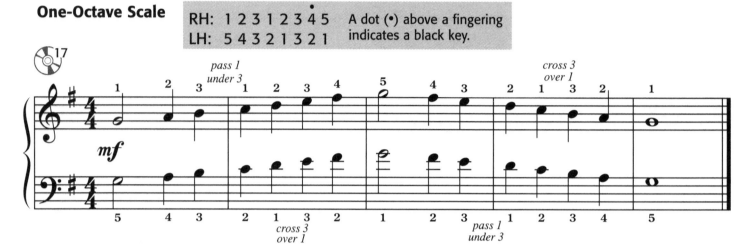

Scale Preparation for Steal Drum Band (pp. 16–17)

Play the examples 3 times each day.

E Minor (1 sharp—F#)

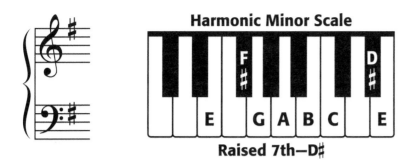

Harmonic Minor Scale

Raised 7th—D#

One-Octave Scale

RH: 1 2 3 1 2 3 4 5 A dot (•) above a fingering
LH: 5 4 3 2 1 3 2 1 indicates a black key.

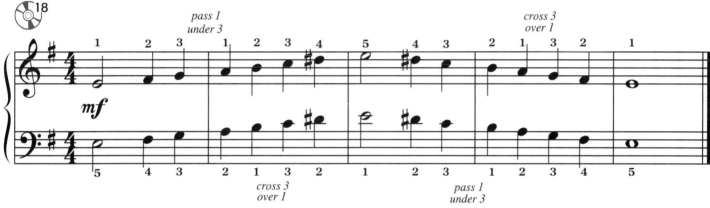

Scale Preparation for Egyptian Journey (pp. 18–19)

Play the examples 3 times each day.

Steel Drum Band

19 Performance Model
20 Practice Tempo (♩ = 112)
21 Performance Tempo (♩ = 126)

Mike Springer

Egyptian Journey

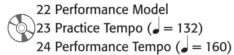

22 Performance Model
23 Practice Tempo (♩ = 132)
24 Performance Tempo (♩ = 160)

Mike Springer

B♭ Major (2 flats—B♭, E♭)

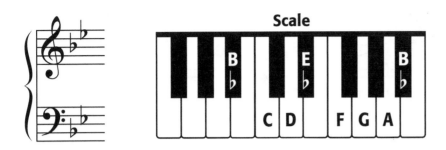

Scale

One-Octave Scale

🔘25

| RH: | 4̇ 1 2 3̇ 1 2 3 4̇ | A dot (•) above a fingering |
| LH: | 3 2 1 4 3 2 1 3 | indicates a black key. |

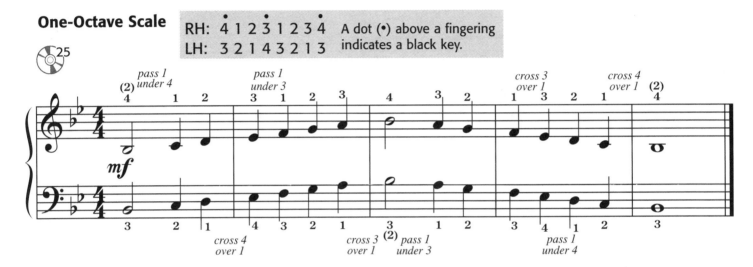

Scale Preparation for Winding River (pp. 22–23)

Play the examples 3 times each day.

G Minor (2 flats—B♭, E♭)

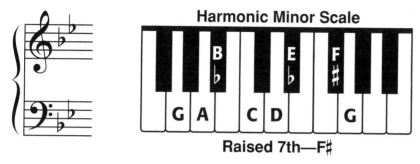

Raised 7th—F♯

One-Octave Scale

🔘 26

RH: 1 2 3 1 2 3 4 5   A dot (•) above a fingering
LH: 5 4 3 2 1 3 2 1   indicates a black key.

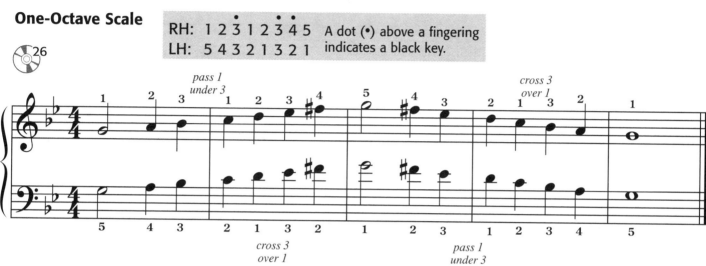

Scale Preparation for Dreaming (pp. 24–25)

Play the examples 3 times each day.

Winding River

27 Performance Model
28 Practice Tempo (♩. = 56)
29 Performance Tempo (♩. = 63)

Mike Springer

Moderately slow and flowing

Dreaming

30 Performance Model
31 Practice Tempo (♩ = 84)
32 Performance Tempo (♩ = 100)

Mike Springer

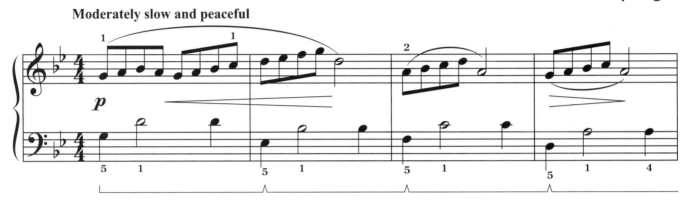

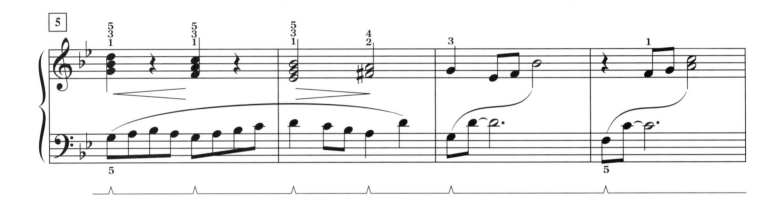

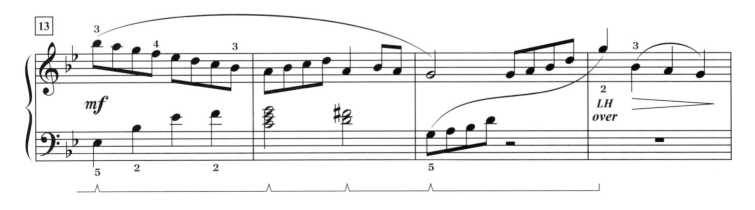

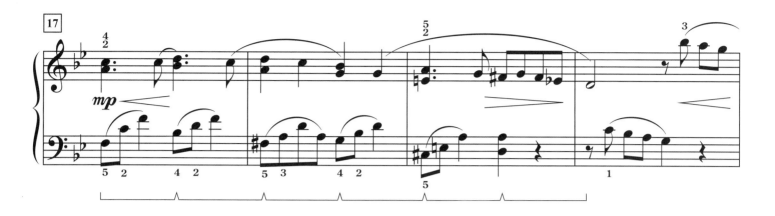

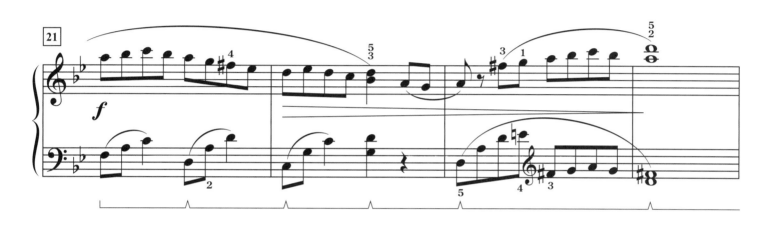

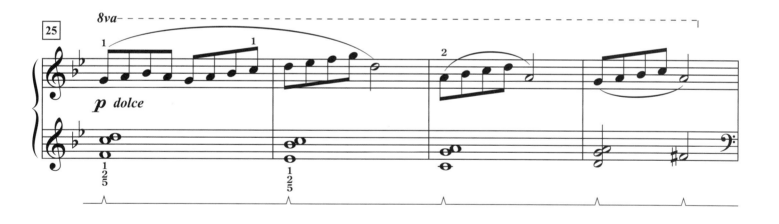

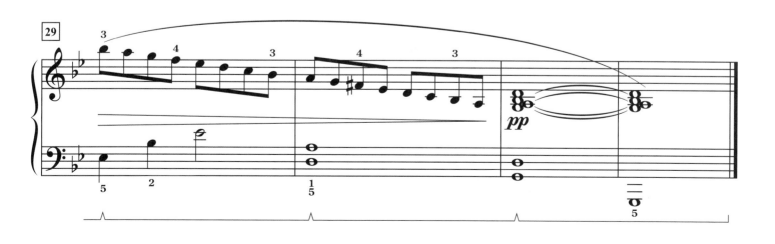

D Major (2 sharps—F♯, C♯)

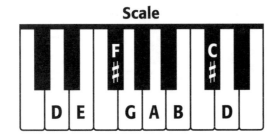

One-Octave Scale

RH: 1 2 3̇ 1 2 3 4 5   A dot (•) above a fingering
LH: 5 4 3 2 1 3 2 1   indicates a black key.

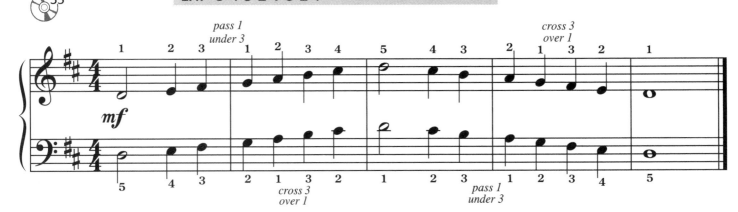

Scale Preparation for Morning Snow (pp. 28–29)

Play the examples 3 times each day.

B Minor (2 sharps—F♯, C♯)

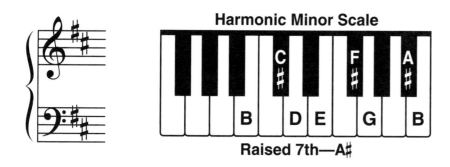

Harmonic Minor Scale

Raised 7th—A♯

One-Octave Scale

RH: 1 2̇ 3 1 2̇ 3 4̇ 5   A dot (•) above a fingering
LH: 4 3 2 1 4 3 2 1   indicates a black key.

34

Scale Preparation for Fleeting Moments (pp. 30–31)

Play the examples 3 times each day.

Morning Snow

35 Performance Model
36 Practice Tempo (♩ = 120)
37 Performance Tempo (♩ = 132)

Mike Springer

Fleeting Moments

38 Performance Model
39 Practice Tempo (♩ = 100)
40 Performance Tempo (♩ = 112)

Mike Springer

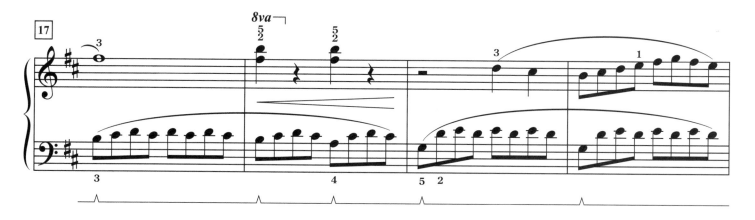

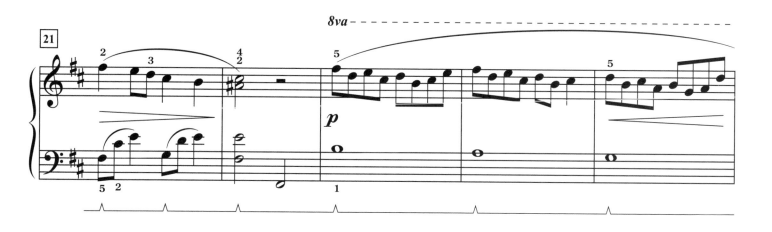